Apr 2017

D1171721

KNOW YOUR BODY

YOUR MUSCLES

By George Fittleworth

Gareth Stevens
PUBLISHING

Please visit our website, www.garethstevens.com. For a free color catalog of all our high-quality books, call toll free 1-800-542-2595 or fax 1-877-542-2596.

Library of Congress Cataloging-in-Publication Data

Fittleworth, George, author.
  Your muscles / George Fittleworth.
      pages cm. — (Know your body)
  Includes bibliographical references and index.
  ISBN 978-1-4824-4457-5 (pbk.)
  ISBN 978-1-4824-4401-8 (6 pack)
  ISBN 978-1-4824-4421-6 (library binding)
  1. Muscles—Juvenile literature. 2. Human physiology—Juvenile literature. I. Title.
  QP321.F485 2017
  612.7'4—dc23

                                2015021479

Published in 2017 by
Gareth Stevens Publishing
111 East 14th Street, Suite 349
New York, NY 10003

Copyright © 2017 Gareth Stevens Publishing

Designer: Andrea Davison-Bartolotta
Editor: Therese Shea

Photo credits: Cover, p. 1 Christopher Futcher/Getty Images; pp. 3, 4, 6, 8, 10, 12, 14, 16, 18, 20, 22–24 Anna Frajtova/Shutterstock.com; p. 5 Jupiterimages/Creatas/ Thinkstock; p. 7 (all main images) blueringmedia/iStock/Thinkstock; p. 7 (background) Lukutina Olesya/Shutterstock.com; p. 9 beyhes/iStock/Thinkstock; p. 11 (main) Monkey Business Images/Monkey Business/Thinkstock; p. 11 (inset) Alila Medical Media/Shutterstock.com; p. 13 (main) Tanya Constantine/Blend Images/Thinkstock; p. 13 (inset) stihii/Shutterstock.com; p. 15 (main) Jupiterimages/Stockbyte/Thinkstock; p. 15 (inset) joshya/Shutterstock.com; p. 17 Sebastian Kaulitzki/Shutterstock.com; p. 19 Viacheslav Nikolaenko/Shutterstock.com; p. 21 monkeybusinessimages/iStock/ Thinkstock.

Printed in the United States of America

CPSIA compliance information: Batch #CS16GS: For further information contact Gareth Stevens, New York, New York at 1-800-542-2595.

CONTENTS

Boldface words appear in the glossary.

Marvelous Muscles

Your body has over 600 muscles. You couldn't move without them. Your heart couldn't beat. You couldn't even think. Your brain is made of muscles, too! Without your muscles, many of your body parts wouldn't work.

Three Kinds

Muscles are made up of **fibers** that can **stretch**. The bigger the muscle, the more fibers it's made of. The human body has three kinds of muscles. They're called skeletal muscles, cardiac muscles, and smooth muscles.

skeletal

cardiac

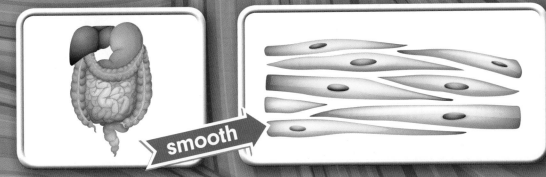

smooth

Skeletal Muscles

Skeletal muscles are the muscles you can feel just below your skin. They're connected to your **skeleton**. They work in pairs. One muscle moves a body part in one direction, and the other muscle moves it in the other direction.

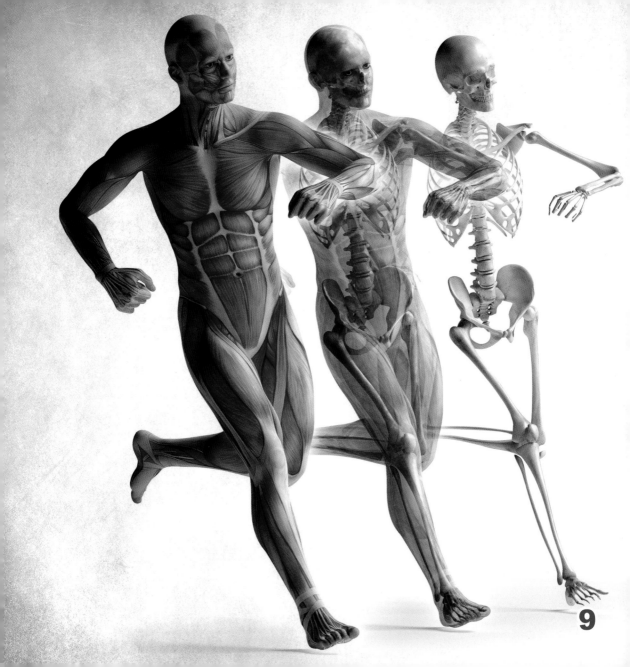

9

Skeletal muscles are the muscles you can control. They're called **voluntary** muscles. When you want to move, your brain sends a message to the muscle along a **motor nerve**. Then, the nerve creates **energy** that moves the muscle.

brain

nerve

muscle

Muscles move the body by contracting and relaxing. Contracting means becoming shorter. The muscle fibers slide together to make a fatter shape. Relaxing means the fibers slide apart. The muscle gets longer and thinner.

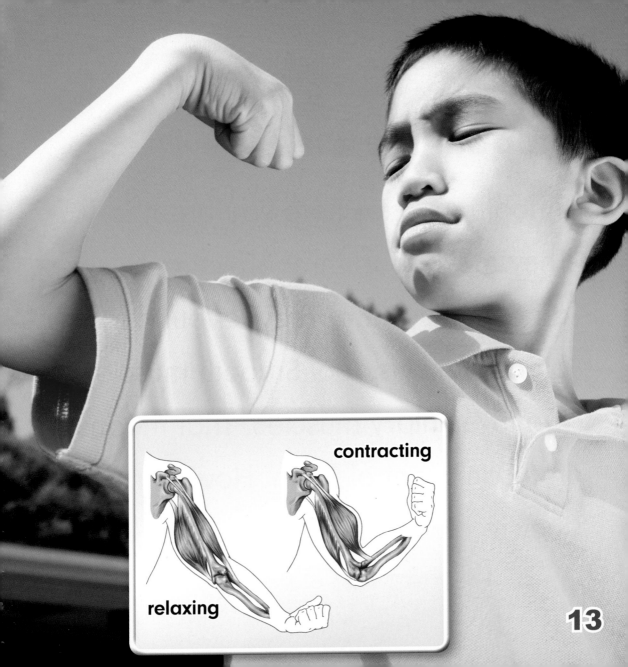

contracting

relaxing

Smooth Muscles

Smooth muscles help you breathe. They move food through your **digestive system**. They're found in **blood vessels**, too. Smooth muscles are involuntary muscles. That means you can't control them. However, they're always at work.

swallowing food

muscles relax →

muscles contract

muscles relax →

15

Cardiac Muscles

Cardiac muscles are found in the heart. The muscles of the heart contract to send blood out to your body parts. They relax to let blood into the heart after it has traveled throughout the body. Cardiac muscles are involuntary, too.

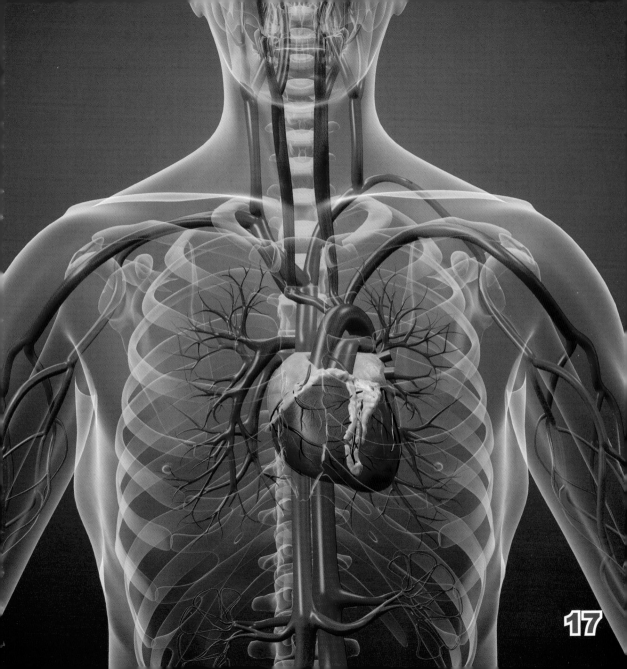

Ouch!

Have you ever had a muscle cramp? That means a muscle has contracted and won't relax. Have you ever had a muscle strain? That's when you stretch a muscle so far that you tear fibers. You must rest so the muscle can mend.

19

Keep Moving!

Eating healthy foods supplies your muscles with energy. You can keep your muscles working well by exercising every day, too. Different activities exercise different muscles. So, keep active in lots of fun ways. Move your muscles!

GLOSSARY

blood vessel: a small tube in the body that carries blood

digestive system: the body's way of breaking down food so it can be used

energy: power used to do work

fiber: a long, thin thread

motor nerve: a part of the body that carries messages from the brain to a muscle

skeleton: the bony frame of the body

stretch: to lengthen or widen

voluntary: doing something by choice or on purpose

FOR MORE INFORMATION

BOOKS

Barraclough, Sue. *The Skeletal and Muscular Systems: How Can I Stand on My Head?* Chicago, IL: Heinemann Library, 2008.

Burstein, John. *The Mighty Muscular and Skeletal Systems: How Do My Bones and Muscles Work?* New York, NY: Crabtree Publishing, 2009.

Manolis, Kay. *Muscular System.* Minneapolis, MN: Bellwether Media, 2009.

WEBSITES

Muscles in the Human Body
www.ducksters.com/science/muscles.php
Read some fun facts about your muscles.

Your Muscles
kidshealth.org/kid/htbw/muscles.html#
Learn names for special muscles in your body.

INDEX